To Bess & Buzz with love

*And I offer this,   that as you read what
I gladly dedicate to you, you may know of
my labors. And, please, as you read, prune the
faults and approve what is good.*

—WALAFRID STRABO, *Hortulus.* AD 840.

Illustrated by MARJORIE STODGELL
Designed by DONNA SICKLESMITH ANDERSON
Copyright © 1992 by STARWOOD PUBLISHING, INC.
All rights reserved.
No part of this book may be reproduced without
the written permission of the publisher.
Printed in Japan by DAI NIPPON
5 4 3 2 1   98 97 96 95 94 93 92

Library of Congress Cataloging-in-Publication Data
Rago, Linda Ours
     The herbal almanac by Linda Ours Rago:
illustrations by Marjorie Stodgell
     ISBN 0-912347-99-6 : $14.95
     1. Herbs—Folklore—Calendar. I. Title
GR780.R34   1992   91-47975
581.6'3--dc20   CIP

The *Herbal* ALMANAC

Written by Linda Ours Rago
Illustrated by Marjorie Stodgell

VOLUME ONE

Starwood Publishing, Inc.
Washington, D.C.

INTRODUCTION

*F*OR MORE THAN twenty years now I have spent part of each day among my herbs. The warm soil and green leaves of Spring and Summer have become as sustaining to me as my breath. The frantic harvest of Autumn is nearly exhausting, but the plants themselves revive my strength to celebrate and share their bounty, first with my family and then with others at an annual harvest fair. In Winter I am sustained by the handful of herb pots on each of my drafty old windowsills where their fragrant presence conjures up premonitions of Summer and warmth.

Gradually I have come to know there is much truth and wisdom in the plant lore passed to us by our forbearers. Rosemary's spicy, musky scent *does* evoke memories of a particular sunlit afternoon in the garden or a special Christmas Eve at home with the family. Lemon balm *does* make me merry again on dull afternoons as I ponder how quickly my children have grown up and my parents have grown older.

I nurture my herbs and they give me the wonder of their magic, sharing an ancient power, one that touches my life and is the force of all living things.

Naturalist Henry Beston wrote that only if we are aware of the earth as poetry do we truly live. Ages and peoples that have severed the growing world from their spirit, he said, find their veins grown hollow and their hearts empty.

*M*OST OF US once were farmers. Green and growing things were the source of our religion, ritual, and song. These little mysteries have all but passed out of our lives as we've moved to the cities and suburbs where great yellow bulldozers have torn out the tangled fencerow. Now we sit before computer terminals or shuffle piles of papers in organizations far from the garden. For many of us who still bring herbs and all plants into our lives and celebrations, herb gardening is a way of reaching the full of human joy.

This book is about the herbs our ancestors brought from England, dark Northern Europe, and the sun-warmed shores of the Mediterranean. We have forgotten much more of them than we know. Let us hold on to the knowledge passed down to us, open ourselves to herbal magic, and make this lore our own again.

Lady Rosalind Northcote was a sensitive Englishwoman who loved the old herb ways. She wrote in 1912, *"Nowadays, when everything travels more quickly along the road of life, the eyes of ordinary mortals get confused with the movement and the jostling and they do not see the pretty by-play that goes on in the bushes by the way, nor peer into the depths of the woodlands beyond."*

I take comfort in knowing the magic of the herb world still exists in quiet corners, and there are still mortals who catch glimpses from the corners of their eyes.

*W*HAT IS AN HERB? The classic definition is a green plant that has been cherished for itself and for a use. There are salad herbs, pot herbs, nose herbs, healing herbs, and magical herbs. Often a single plant crosses over from pot herb to healing herb or nose herb to magic herb on one warm afternoon. Some herbs are not aromatic, more gray than green, and many aren't fit to eat. But each has its place in our green inheritance, our ritual, our religion, and our song. The boundaries of an herb garden are as long as our imaginations and as wide as the mysteries of our souls.

*T*HE ESSENCE of these plants was once held in a different light from our own. We are very pragmatic today. We think we must eat or drink of a plant to enjoy its benefits, smell or see a plant to enjoy its beauty. Until only a few hundred years ago, our kind knew that by having certain plants around us, their properties would be imparted to us.

Some herbs were considered magical because of their uses in spells and sorcery, others because of powers held within themselves. Our ancestors attributed human-like personalities or spirits to plants in ways we find ludicrous today. Could they have been closer to the truth than we know? *"Rue dislikes basil,"* wrote the ancient Greek, Pliny, in 100 BC, *"but Rue and figs are in a great league and amitie together."* In Italy little sandwiches of figs, walnuts, and a rue leaf are still eaten on holidays.

"Radish is at enmetie with Hyssop," wrote Sir Francis Bacon. Today we call this companion planting, but the theory is the same.

*B*ECAUSE PLANTS were given credit for strong feelings, we can easily understand our forbearers who felt herbs could be sympathetic to their surroundings. Honesty (Lunaria) thrives in an honest woman's garden; where rosemary flourishes, the mistress rules; sage will fade with the fortunes of the household and revive with its good luck.

It is only another small step to understand how a four-leaved clover will enable the bearer to see the witches and how garlic can avert the evil eye.

There was a strong belief that herbs used by magicians for evil were also powerful against that evil. Dill was able to "hinder witches of their will" although it was a favorite among them.

*K*EY INGREDIENTS in almost all of the old spells that survived from pre-Christian Europe included: Pennyroyal, henbane, chervil, vervain, poppy, mandrake, hemlock, and dittany. Herbs particularly liked by the devil were yarrow, ground ivy, and houseleeks. They were also the herbs used to divine the future, dispel evil, and give protection from it.

Much of our herbal knowledge has been lost because it was dangerous to hold the ancient secrets. Poor Elspeth Reoch in the late 18th century was brought to trial in Germany for curing distempers in children by resting on her right knee while pulling up yarrow between her middle finger and thumb and saying, *"In nomen Patris, Filii et Spiritus Sancti."* (In the name of the Father, Son and Holy Spirit.)

*H*ERBS AND FLOWERS have always been sacred to us. Fortuatus, Bishop of Poitiers in the 16th century, wrote: *"When winter binds the earth with ice, all the glory of the field perished with its flowers. But in the spring-time when the Lord overcame Hell, bright grass shoots up and buds come forth . . . Gather these first-fruits and you bear them to the churches and wreath the altars with them . . . gems and incense bow before them."*

The circle of seasons has turned since time began, casting our celebrations and festivals in a pattern as gracefully predictable as the rays of a sunflower. For our ancestors the almanac was indispensable. It gave them not only a calendar of feasts and saint's days, it also let them know just when to expect the waning or waxing moon and the seasonal rotation of the stars. To farming people, these were events of great importance. To gardeners, they are still events worthy of more than passing notice. When we plant and harvest and celebrate in harmony with the great wheel of seasons, our gardens still flourish, and we grow in wisdom and contentment.

Growing and using herbs has been our way of relating to this awesome universe. Herbal lore carries prognostications of weather and romance, cures, and protection from things that go bump in the night.

$\mathcal{T}$HIS ALMANAC IS ABOUT the magic of plants. Its sources are many — earnest words from friends and family, ancient herbals with worn vellum pages and old handwritten recipes. Some of it is practical, some of it is eccentric. Much of the information is of no use, but all of it is fascinating. Let us revive some of these charming rituals of the past. Our family has found merriment in setting out little dishes of moss on May Eve to entice the wee folk back into our garden. When my husband

travels, I usually slip a few well-chosen seeds into his pocket for protection. My lovely daughter's cheeks were often washed in the dew of lady's mantle when she was a baby, and now we tuck sprigs of mint into the care-package sent to our son in college. Wassailing the apple tree on Twelfth Night is a good excuse for inviting the neighbors over to brighten a dull January evening as well as insuring a bountiful harvest. At the Summer Solstice we gather with friends to share a potluck supper of salads and divine our futures through the firelit vervain.

It doesn't matter whether the long history of herbal magic shows we are susceptible to suggestion or that we simply believe in what has not yet been explained. Herb magic is enchanting!

—LINDA OURS RAGO

NOTE: *There will be many references to dates "old style" or "new style". These refer to the addition Pope Gregory XIII made in 1582. He added ten days to the old calendar introduced by Julius Caesar in 45 BC. To add to the confusion, much of Catholic Europe adopted the "new style" while Protestant Britain and her colonies held the "old style" until 1752. Much of the information for this almanac was compiled during this confusing time.*

JANUARY

1

New Year's Day presents are omens for success in the coming year. The traditional gift is, *"an orenge or lymon stickt round about with cloaves."*
—THOMAS LUPTON, 1598

In Wales it was proper to give a New Year's gift of a *calennig*, a clove-studded orange impaled upon a rowan tree skewer. *Strenia*, the customary gifts that Romans exhanged on the Kalends of January were bay branches and palm fronds for a year of joy and happiness.

2

It is traditional to burn twigs of sweet-smelling marjoram as kindling in January.

3

Highlanders burn juniper this time of year. This holiday celebration has much in common with the ancient Roman Saturnalia, the festival of Janus, the two-faced god.

4

*"Of trembling winter, the fairest flowers o' th'
     season
Are our carnations and streak'd gillyvors..."*
—SHAKESPEARE,
     The Winter's Tale, Act IV, Perdita

TWELFTHNIGHT EVE

5

Christmas Eve, Old Style
On this night the Holy Thorn at Glastonbury blooms.

TWELFTHNIGHT

6

This is the traditional end of the Christmas Festival, Epiphany. A cake was served in which a dried bean was hidden. Whoever found the bean was the Bean Cake King and ruled over the wassailing festivities. Today is the time to wassail the apples trees,
*"Health to Thee, good apple tree
Well to bear pocket-fulls, hat-fulls,
Peck fulls, bushel bag-fulls"*
If one neglects this ritual, there will be a poor crop of apples this year. It is the day to drink old cider and feast upon caraway cakes in honor of the apple goddess Pomona.

Today is the day to take down the Christmas greens — always gently to burn or lay about the garden as winter mulch.

OPPOSITE: *lavender and loveage;* ABOVE: *rosemary.*

JANUARY

7

This is the traditional day to begin work after Christmas.
"If maids a-spinning go,
Burn the flax and bring in the tow."
—HERRICK, *Hesperides.* 1648

8

It is a good time to make herb bread. Herbalist Plimy described the ancient Greek use of poppy seed, *"Country people sprinkle poppy seed on the uppermost crust of their bread, making it adhere by means of the yolk of eggs, the under crust being seasoned with parsley and girth to heighten the flavor of flour."*

9

Winter Cockle-warmer
is an old name for a winter
soup. Make a cockle-warmer more savory with dried calendula blossoms, winter savory, lovage, chives and rosemary.

PLOUGH DAY
10

It was traditional for boys called "plough witches" to parade through the village on Plough Day. First ploughing could often be done now in Northern England. A plough trimmed with herbs and ribbons was often pulled through the village. Bessie, a carica-ture of Freya the Norse goddess, was queen of the day.

11

New Year's Eve, Old Style
Beware of "docken stalks." Witches used them to strike down enemies.

12

Groundsel blooms now. Shepherds Purse blooms now. It *"stayeth bleeding in a part of the body, whether the juice be drunk, poultice wise or in bath."*
—JOHN GERARD, *Herbal.* 1633

ABOVE: *loveage* (9) and *parsley* (11).

JANUARY

13

This was the first day to be married after the Christmas ban. The house could be decked up with wedding herbs now: sage, lavender, jasmine, marjoram, and borage.

14

If you are single greet the first new moon after New Year's by standing astride the bars of the garden gate and saying:
"All hail to the Moon
Hail to thee
I prithee good moon reveal to me
This night who my wife (or husband) must be."
—JOHN AUBREY, *Miscellanies.* 1695

15

"Thy garden twifallow, 'stroy hemlock and mallow."
—THOMAS TUSSER, 1557

16

For hiccups on this day, *"Take three or four preserv'd damsons (plums) in your mouth at a time and swallow them by degrees."*
—E. SMITH, *Compleat Housewife.* 1744

17

Twelfthnight, Old Style.
Make merry!

18

On this day read *Herbs and the Earth* written by Henry Beston in 1935. It is the best book about herbs and people and the universe.

ABOVE: *hemlock.*

JANUARY

19

The sun enters the house of Aquarius. Special herbs for those born under this sign are: alder leaves for refreshment, violets to dry up watery humours, hyssop to take away pains in the head and strengthen all parts of the body, and mint to invigorate.

ST. AGNES EVE

20

This is the night to conduct love divinations. Maids scattered barley seeds under apple trees saying,

"Barley, Barley I sow thee
That my true love I may see,
Taketh thy rake and follow me."

Her future husband walked along behind her, taking up the barley seed with his rake.

ST. AGNES DAY

21

Agnes is the patron saint of young girls. Today maids acquired sweethearts. To do so they must carry ivy leaves next to their breasts, fast the day before, put on clean nightclothes and go to sleep saying,

"Fair Saint Agnes, play thy part,
And send me my own sweetheart,
Not in his best nor worst array,
But in clothes he wears everyday;
That tomorrow I may him ken,
From among all other men."

22

This is the traditional day to plant new hedges.

23

When feeding your winter birds, note the tiny thistle seed and remember its ancient heritage. In England it is actually called Thistlefinch because the finches love it so. The thistle was thought to be a talisman against the plague and it cured "diseases of melancholy."

24

Try making Rosie Atkins' homemade cleansing cream for chapped winter skin.

"Half an ounce of beeswax, half an ounce of emulsifying wax, four ounces of petroleum jelly, one ounce of witch hazel and three ounces of rosewater. Melt the waxes and petroleum jelly in a double boiler, stirring, and gradually add the other liquids."

ABOVE: *hyssop.*

JANUARY

25

This is the feast of the conversion of St. Paul. Good weather foretells a good gardening year.

26

Wear a scarlet nightcap stitched up with lavender to shun winter melancholy.

27

Germander is an evergreen herb that can be brought into the house today. It was a traditional strewing herb, and herbalist Nicolas Culpeper wrote of it, *"...it is a most prevalent herb of Mercury and strengthens the brain and apprehension exceedingly."* Germander is the traditional herb knot garden border.

28

Wear garlic or asafoeida about your neck to keep away the winter flu.

29

Keep a pot of catnip in the windowsill for the house cat in winter. The adage is
*"If you set it, the cats will get it.
If you sow, the cats won't know it."*

30

To ward off nightmares from the long winter nights, try aniseed, licorice and garlic.

31

The full moon of January is the Wolf Moon. Protect the house with hound's tongue and wolfsbane tonight.

ABOVE: *germander* (27) and *catnip* (29).

FEBRUARY

1

This was the Celtic feast of awakening.
The pagan Brigit is associated with fertility
and the female power of regeneration.
Straw effigies of Brigit and her white cow
come to life on this day only.

The first day of Spring in the gardener's year.

CANDLEMAS DAY

2

This celebrated the Purification
of the Virgin Mary. Candles and
mullein tapers were lit and carried in pro-
cessions. It was the day to bless the candles
and torches. The consecrated candles were
a powerful charm all year.

It is also the traditional day to take down the
last of the Christmas greens. For every green
leaf left in the house after Candlemas, a
malicious goblin will pay the house a visit
and do mischief.

"Down with the Rosemary and so
Down with the Baies and mistletoe;
Down with Holly, Ivie, all
Wherewith ye dress the Christmas Hall;
That so the superstitions find
No one Least branch there left behind;
For look how many leaves there be
Neglected there (maids, trust to me)
So many goblins you shall see."
—HERRICK, *Hesperides.* 1648

The Greek goddess Persephone returns to the
light of her mother Demeter after her descent
into darkness. It was the old Roman custom
on this day to burn mullein tapers to the
goddess Februa.

ST. BLAISE DAY

3

The saint miraculously cured a
boy with a bone in his throat so the day was
named after him. Herbs to soothe a sore
throat are hyssop, horehound, and sage.

4

Gather snowdrops
today to purify the
house. Folk names are
Fair Maids, Candlemas
Bells, and Snow Piercers.

5

Purple-flowered Lady Thistle was used to
decorate churches now. The white spots on
the leaves were thought to have been marked
by the Virgin's milk.

ST. DOROTHEA'S DAY

6

In the 4th century in Caesarea a young girl
was picking roses when a young man rode by.
He was a handsome young Roman sent out
by the Governor to kill all Christians. The
young Roman was enchanted by Dorothea's
beauty and asked for a rose. She gave him a
great bunch of herbs and roses and other
flowers, and he rode away in love with her.
    When he was interrogating people ac-
cused of Christianity, among the crowd was
lovely Dorothea. The Roman was terribly
upset and tried to persuade her to deny her
religion. She refused. The young Roman said,
"Bride of Christ, send me a gift of flowers when
you gain your beloved." That night, after
Dorothea was killed, an angel came to him
in his dreams with armfuls of roses and herbs.
He was converted to Christianity, and also
killed by the Romans.

OPPOSITE: *scented geranium, rosemary, ivy, and rosa rugosa;* ABOVE: *sage.*

FEBRUARY

7

"Sow mustard seed,
and helpe to kill weed,
Where sets doo growe,
see nothing ye sowe."
    —THOMAS TUSSER, *Five Hundred*
    Points of Good Husbandry. 1573

8

A perfect day for an herbal bath. Comfrey, sage, bay, parsley, and orange peel help the skin feel healthy. Lovage will make one lovable. *"...goats milk infused with violets, and there is not a young prince on earth who will not be charmed with thy beauty."*
    —An old Gaelic saying about the bath.

9

Plan for a scented garden. Among the sweet-scented herbs that easily give up their fragrance are lavender, lemon verbena, the scented geraniums, nicotiana, clove pinks, rosemary, old roses, and thyme.

10

Serve up a savory stew today, and flavor it with a bouquet garni. A bouquet garni always includes a bay leaf, parsley, thyme, basil, savory, marjoram, and chervil tied up in a little bag. Remember to remove the bouquet garni before serving a dish.

11

Today is the day to clear brush from the fenceline and *"set for thy pot, best herbes to be got."*
    —16th-century rhyme

12

Today the alder tree catkins appear.
"Alder leaves gathered while morning dew is on them, brought into a chamber troubled with fleas, will gather them thereunto; which being suddenly cast out, will rid the chamber of these troublesome bedfellows."
    —NICOLAS CULPEPER, *Herbal.* 1633

ABOVE: *comfrey.*

FEBRUARY

13

Winter is nearly over.
"Feb, fill the dike,
With what thou dost like.
Forgotten month past,
Do now at the last."
—Thomas Tusser, 1573

ST. VALENTINE'S DAY

14

This was also Lupercalia of ancient Rome, when couples drew names from a bag and were paired for the festival.

There is an old belief that the birds choose mates this day. From this belief, no doubt, we get the idea this is the day for romance. Pin a sweet bay leaf at each corner of your pillow and another in the center. If you dream of your true love, your are sure to be married before the year ends.

Some herbal aphrodisiacs are cyclamen, lettuce, pansies, periwinkle, bay, marigolds, thyme, wormwood, marjoram, coriander, clove, cinnamon, ginger, lavender, rose, borage, rocket, garden cress, artichokes, parsley, carrot, dill, anise, and chervil.

15

"In February in the New of the Moon, sow
borage, coriander, marjoram, radish, rosemary
and sorrel."
—Gervase Markham,
The English Housewife. 1683

16

Sometimes this is Shrove Tuesday. This is the time for confessing sin. "Shrive" is the Saxon word for confession. It is the traditional day for eating pancakes. *"The pancake bell is rung on Shrove Tuesday at nine a.m. in 'which cookes do mingle with water, egges, spice; and other tragicall magicall inchantments'"*
—Taylor, the Water Poet, 1630

17

Sometimes this is the beginning of Lent, Ash Wednesday. The word Lent comes from the Anglo-Saxon *"when days lengthen."* It is traditional to fast during this time: *"But onyons, browne bread, leeks and salt must now poor men daily gnaw."*

18

A Jack-a-Lent is a puppet used as a scarecrow now.

ABOVE: *savory* (13) and *wood sorrel* (18).

FEBRUARY

19

Coltsfoot flowers appear. A folkname is "poorman's baccy." *"The fume of dried leaves taken through a funnel effectually helpeth those that are troubled with coughs and shortness of breath and fetch their wind thick and often. Being taken in this manner as this take tobacco, it mightily prevaileth."*
—JOHN GERARD, *Herbal.* 1633

20

The sun enters the house of Pisces today. Herbs to especially promote the well-being of those born under this sign are: alder leaves gathered while morning dew is on them and brought into a chamber to cast out trouble, chamomile to take away weariness, lavender for all griefs and pains of the head and mint to invigorate.

21

A birch twig is given by a woman to a man as a sign of romantic interest. If she wishes to discourage a man, she will give him a hazel twig.

22

Myrtle bushes planted on either side of the front door ensure peace and love in the home.

23

"If you marry in Lent, you will live to repent." Eat celery to subdue the urge to wed.

24

Today is the ancient Roman festival of Terminalia when farmers placed garlands of grain and herbs on boundary stones.

ABOVE: *chamomile.*

FEBRUARY

25

The first violets appear in sunny, sheltered places. *"Violets have great perogative above others, not only because the mind conceiveth a certain pleasure and recreation by smelling and handling these most odoriferous flowers, but also for that very many by these violets receive ornament and comely grace; for there be made of them garlands for the head, nosegays, posies, which are delightful to look on and pleasant to smell to."*
—JOHN GERARD, *Herbal.* 1633

26

To induce dreams of a future husband or wife, pick nine holly leaves on a Friday at midnight and place them in a three-cornered cloth under the pillow. The charm only works if absolute silence is kept between the moment the leaves are gathered and the first light of dawn.

27

If you have a winter cold try this. *"Herbal bathes for colds. Of this wise ought they to be bathed dry which have taken cold, before they do bath in water. Take mugwort, sage, fennel, pennyroyal of a handful; chop them small and put them in two bags and seethe them. Then put the water the herbs have been sodden in a tub, and set thy feet therein as hot as ye can suffer it. Lay one bag under and sit thereupon; and lay the other upon your stomach reaching down to your privy members. But look the bags be not too hot."*
—JOHN HOLLYBUSH,
The Homish Apothecary. 1561

28

Aspen trees bloom now. *"Aspen tree, and may also be called Tremble, after the French name, considering it is the matter whereof women's tongues were made (as the poets and some others report), which seldom cease wagging."*
—JOHN GERARD, *Herbal.* 1633

A folk name for the aspen is Quickbeam, and the legend is that it was used to make the wood for Christ's cross and has never ceased to tremble.

29
LEAP YEAR / ST. JOB'S DAY
(once every four years)

This is the unluckiest day of the year! It is unlucky because Job cursed the day he was born. Wear a sprig of rue as protection today.

NOTES

MARCH

I

Gwyl Dewi Sant, the patron saint of Wales lived to be 104 years old. Leeks are worn this day to celebrate the Welshmen's victory over the Saxons. In the year 1533 an old tome read, *"Davyd of Wales Loveth Lekes."* In London "Welshmen" made of gingerbread are made in bakeshops and sold today.

This is also Vesta, the Roman holiday when withered bays were withdrawn from the Vestal hearth, and it was dressed with fresh ones. The Vestal fire was rekindled.

2

Lide is the month of March in the west of England. *"Eate leeks in Lide, and Ramsins in May, And all the year after Physicians may play."*

3

Crocus is now in bloom. In William Shakespeare's time saffron referred to the common yellow crocus, and it represented the color yellow. *"No, no, no, your son was misled with a snipt-taffeta fellow there, whose villainous Saffron would have made all the umbaked and doughy youth of a nation in his colour."*
    —SHAKESPEARE,
    All's Well That Ends Well, Act IV, *Lafeu*

4

Herbalist Thomas Tusser says this is a good time to manure the garden.

5

March Hares were especially unlucky to meet when setting out on a journey. If you saw one, you must call it a nickname like Wat or old Malkin. These March Hares were really shape-shifting witches. Protection from them was assured by placing vervain or rowan leaves on a gunstock and shooting them with a silver bullet.

6

*"If apples bloom in March,
In vain for 'un you'll sarch."*

OPPOSITE: *ivy and crocus;* ABOVE: *vervain.*

MARCH

7

Primroses (or cowslips) are in bloom now. An old tradition was for young girls to tie up a bunch of sixty flower clusters into a "cucking ball." The girls tossed the ball to one another calling out, *"Titsy, totsy, tell me true, Who shall I be married to?"* Each girl was chosen in turn and the name of local bachelors called out. The last name to be called before the ball was dropped would be the girl's mate.

8

"In March, the moon being new, sow Garlic, Chervil, Marjoram, White Poppy, Double Marigolds, Thyme and Violets. At full moon Chicory, Fennel and Apples of Love. At the wane, Artichokes, Basil, Cucumbers, Spinach, Gillyflowers, Cabbage, Lettuce, Burnets, Leeks and Savory."
—GERVASE MARKHAM,
The English Housewife. 1683

9

Now you can sow peas and plant potatoes. *"Plant your 'taturs when you will, They won't come up before April."*

10

Warts can be removed by rubbing them with a green pea. Then bury the pea, and as it rots the warts will disappear.

11

Nettle leaves are greening. *"If you lightly touch a nettle, It will sting you for your pains. But grasp it, like a lad of mettle — soft as silk it will remain."* (An old ditty from Ireland) Nettles are a spring green rich in iron. Boil and drain them twice before eating them. This takes out the sting — and probably the iron!

12

Wearing fresh pea blossoms attracts people and promotes friendships.

ABOVE: *basil* (8) and *cowslips* (10).

MARCH

13

Mothering Sunday often falls near this date. It occurs on the 4th Sunday of Lent and comes from the scripture, *"Jerusalem, mother of us all."* It is the traditional day for children to give violets and rosemary to mothers. Also cakes of saffron were brought to mothers and grandmothers on this day.

14

Blue periwinkles are sometimes blooming by this day. *"It is a tradition with many that a wreath made of Periwinkle and bound about the legs, defendeth them from cramp. Periwinkle leaves eaten by man and wife together cause love — which is a rare quality indeed, if it be true."*
—WILLIAM COLES, *Adam in Eden.* 1657

IDES OF MARCH
15

Beware of ill omens. Wear vervain and St. Johnswort. *"...a maiden over whom Satan had no power as long as she had vervaine and St. Johns grass about her."*
—JACKSON'S *Works.* 1673

16

The delicate anemone is in bloom. *"Youth, like a thin Anemome, displays His silken leaf, and in a morn decays."*
—SIR WILLIAM JONES, 1810

ST. PATRICK'S DAY
17

Christians found symbolism of the Holy Trinity in the shamrock's three leaves. St. Patrick plucked the shamrock and said, *"Is it not possible for the Father, Son and Holy Ghost as for these three leaves to grow upon a single stock?"* Druids found other three-leaved plants sacred as well.

18

Winter savory is budding now. It was added to dishes to aid in digestion and applied externally to ease the sting of bees. *"Mercury claims dominion over this herb. Keep it by you all year, if you love yourself and your ease, and it is a hundred pounds to a penny if you do not."*
—NICOLAS CULPEPER, 1653

ABOVE: *St. Johnswort.*

MARCH

19

Children born today are especially lucky. If the weather is fair, it will be a good year for gardening.

Quinquatrus, the birthday of Roman goddess Minerva, so named because it was celebrated five days after the Ides of March. Winners of games and races wore crowns of olives which were sacred to Minerva.

20

The first mint leaves are up. *"Come see my mint, my fine green mint,"* is an old London street cry. In mythology, Mintha, mint's namesake, was a beautiful nymph who loved Pluto, god of the underworld. In a jealous rage, Persephone changed her into the small mint plant who has ever since lived in the shady places of the dark world of Pluto.

SPRING EQUINOX
21

This is the Spring Equinox!

The sun enters the house of Aries today. Herbs to promote the well-being of those born under Aries include cowslips to restore lost beauty (also a remedy against false apparitions and frenzies).

Artemisian was the ancient Greek month of March. Wear a sprig of artemisia in honor of the moon goddess.

22

The first daffodils bloom now. *"When daffodils begin to peer, With heigh! the doxy over the dale, Why, then comes in the sweet o' the year; For the red blood reigns in the winter's pale."*

— SHAKESPEARE,
The Winter's Tale, Act IV.

23

Recipe for Lenten Fish: *"Stuff with a lump of butter and mace, parsley, savory thyme, minced small."*

— GERVASE MARKHAM,
The English Housewife. 1683

ST. GABRIEL'S DAY
24

St. Gabriel is the patron saint of messengers. Mugwort and all the artemisias should be worn by letter carriers and messengers to prevent fatigue.

ABOVE: *marigold* (19) and *tarragon* (24).

MARCH

25

This was the first day of the new year to our ancestors in the very dim past. Here is an ancient supplication to the Lady:

"Erce, Erce, Erce, Mother of Earth
May the All-wielder, Ever-Lord grant thee
Acres waxing, growing upwards,
Pregnant with corn, plenteous in strength;
Hosts of grain shafts and glittering plants!
Of broad barley the blossoms
And of white wheat ears waxing,
Of the whole earth the harvest!
Let be guarded the grain against spells
That are sown over the land by sorcery-men:
Nor let cunning woman change it, nor a
*   crafty man."*

26

The early tulips are up. *"Tulips...are esteemed especially for the beauty of their floures. The roots preserved with sugar, or otherwise dresse may be eaten, and are no unpleasant nor any offensive meat, but rather good a nourishing."*
—JOHN GERARD, *Herbal.* 1633

27

Sometimes Palm Sunday falls near this day. Boxwood and flowers and herbs were often used instead of palms in imitation of those carried in procession by the Jews as Christ came into Jerusalem.

Palm Sunday crosses were made of the greens hung up in homes to give protection all year. Willow boughs and willow catkins were traditionally worn on Palm Sunday as well.

28

Willows are in leaf by now. *"Wylowe tree — if a drynke of hit, he shall gete no sones, but only bareyne daughters."*
—BARTHOLOMEUS DE PREPRIET

Willows were also traditionally worn to ward off storms. But to wear willow on other occasions meant a lover was forsaken by the other.

29

"A windy dry March is good for the garden but bad for old-folks and child-bearing women."
—DOVE'S *Almanac.* 1607

30

Ground ivy blooms now. It also is called Gill-go-by-the-hedge, Gill-over-the-ground, blue ivy and alehoff. *"Ground ivy is commended against the humming noises and ringing sound of the ears being put into them, and for them that are hard of hearing."*
—JOHN GERARD, *Herbal.* 1633

31

Gardens of Adonis are little pots sown with fennel and flowers by Sicilian women this time of year.

ABOVE: *lemon balm.*

APRIL

APRIL FOOL'S DAY

1

It is also known as All Fools Day.

"A custom prevails everywhere among us on the First of April, when everybody strives to make as many fools as he can."
—BRAND'S *Antiquities.* 1853

The Roman holiday of Quirinalia also occurred at this time and was called the Feast of Fools. A traditional prank is to send one on an impossible task such as going for fern seed or to find the book entitled *The Life of Eve's Mother.*

ST. URBAN'S DAY

2

St. Urban's Day is the traditional time to take purges or spring tonics. *"A purging ale to be taken in April. Take Strongest ale you can get, and leave in it a bag of crushed senna, polypody of oak, bay berries, ash keys, aniseeds and fennel seeds: Drink thereof about a pint morning and evening. It purgeth the body mightily."*

—*Mrs. Harrington's Book,* 18th century

Today was Veneralia in ancient Rome. Married women invoked Venus to ensure passion. The first rose of the season was worn in her honor.

3

Sometimes this is Maundy Thursday. This comes from the Latin "mandatum" a command. Christ commanded followers to be humble by washing the feet of the disciples. It was customary to wash as many feet in lavender water as the years of one's age.

4

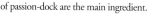

Sometimes this is Good Friday. It was traditional to eat an herb pudding in which the leaves of passion-dock are the main ingredient.

Ancient Greeks offered cakes called *bous* to the moon goddess Diana near this day. They were marked with a cross to symbolize the four quarters of the moon.

5

Passion Sunday sometimes comes now. (5th Sunday in Lent) Passion puddings were made with adderwort, passion dock, nettles, and onions.

6

This is the time for traditional Pace Eggs or Peace Eggs. Boil eggs in gorse bloom for yellow eggs, cochineal for red, onion skin or nettle root for yellow-green, and pasque flower for bright green.

OPPOSITE: *tansy, pansy and parsley;* ABOVE: *lavender.*

APRIL

7

Sometimes this is Easter Eve. This is the traditional time to quench all household fires and light them anew.

"Three great garlands for the crosses of roses and lavender...Three dozen other garlands for the quire."
—Recorded this day in the 16th century from *Disbursements for St. Mary-at-Mill*

8

Sometimes Easter Sunday falls on this day. It is traditional to rise in time to see the sun dance at Easter morn.

This day is celebrated to commemorate the Resurrection of Christ, the Festival of Spring, and rebirth. The Saxon goddess Eostra (whose sacred animal was the rabbit) was worshipped at this time of year. The word "oster" means "to rise" in old Saxon. As late as 1511 it was called Goddus Sunday in country places.

"The hauc shall this day be arrayed with green herbes and swete floures strowde alle aboute — machen clene the houce."
—*The Liber Festival*

Radish root is traditionally eaten on Easter Day *"against the quartan ague."*
—*1565 Manuscript*

9

New potatoes are sometimes up by now.
"Potatoes of Virginia stop fluxes of the bowel and restore Pining Complaints, increase seed and provoke lust, causing fruitfulness in both sexes."
—WILLIAM SALMON, *Herbal.* 1710

Potatoes were forbidden in Burgundy where they were thought to cause leprosy.
—JOHN GERARD, *Herbal.* 1633

10

This is a good day to make candied flowers and herbs. *"Cut flower stalks short, boil sugar with rosewater until it will roll between your thumb and finger. Cool. Dip flowers or herbs into them and dry in a sieve."*
—THOMAS JERMIER

11

Predict the weather by emerging new leaves.
*"Oak before Ash
We'll have a splash
Ash before Oak
We're in for a soak."*

12

To cure a love-sick maid, let her carry basil and rosemary, or; *"Take earthworms, open them, wash them clean, dry them in ovens and dry them to a powder. Give thereof two spoonfuls in white wine in the morning."*
—*Fairfax Household Book,* 17th century

ABOVE: *purslane.*

APRIL

13

Jack-in-the pulpit blooms today. Other country names are Cuckoo Pintle, Dog Cocks, Lords and Ladies, Wake Robin, Stallions and Mares. The jack-in-the-pulpit plant is highly corrosive and toxic. It was sometimes made into a dangerous brew thought to be an aphrodisiac.

14

To keep the rabbits out of the parsley patch, before going to bed say, *"Hares, Hare"* on arising say, *"Rabbits Rabbit."*

15

The Roman festival Tellus Mater celebrated mother earth to ensure plenty during the year. Today is the best day to plant anything!

16

Sometimes this is the second Tuesday after Easter. It is often called Hoke Day, and it is the best day for a wedding. In fact, in Germany the word "Hockzeit" means wedding day.

17

"If apples bloom in April, Why then they'll be plentiful."

18

Make a borage salad to encourage good spirits and courage. Use the new borage seedlings, violet flowers, dandelion leaves, and new lettuce.

ABOVE: *Jack-in-the-pulpit;* (13) and *borage* (18).

APRIL

19

"Sweete April showers, Doo spring Maie flowers. Forgotten month past, Doe now at the last."
—THOMAS TUSSER, *Five Hundred Points of Good Husbandry.* 1573

20

Pansies, one of the oldest favorites in the garden, are in bloom. *"And there is Pansies — that's for thoughts."*
—SHAKESPEARE, *Hamlet*, Act IV

The Anglo-Saxon name was Banwort and the French call it Pensees, or thoughts. It is also known as Love-in-idleness and was once thought to cure an ailing heart. Heartsease was a country name.

21

Ancient Roman festival Palilia in honor of the goddess Pales. This rural deity was celebrated by burning olive, pine, and laurel boughs.

The sun enters the house of Taurus. Herbs especially for the well-being of those born under Taurus are lovage to soothe inward pain, catnip to ease giddiness and pains in the heat, figwort to prevent freckles and chamomile to take away weariness.

22

Thyme is late to green in the Spring, but by now the little leaves are green and fragrant.
"I know a bank where the wild Thyme blows, Where Oxslips and the nodding Violet grows."
—SHAKESPEARE, *Midsummer Night's Dream*, Act II

23

The first roses bloom today! St. George's Day. It is traditional to wear blue and beware of dragons. Bonfires (bonefires) were lit to drive away dragons today — the one thing they fear most.

24

Cowslips are still in bloom. They are the traditional beauty aid. *"An ointment of cowslips takes away spots and wrinkles of the skin. sunburning, freckles, and adds beauty exceedingly."*
—NICOLAS CULPEPER, *Herbal.* 1653.

ABOVE: *chamomile* (19) and *catnip* (24).

APRIL

ST. MARK'S DAY

25

This is a day for feasting and blessing of the grain. Hollybushes were planted in front of houses of those hosting the merry-making.

Robigalia is the ancient Roman rite to appease the mildew spirit to prevent it from attacking the grain. It was celebrated on this day.

26

Crane's bill or wild geranium comes into bloom now. It was once used to ward off the plague and *"The iuyce being inwardly taken is good to heale wounds."*
—JOHN GERARD, *Herbal.* 1633

27

The great and colorful crown imperial is king of the garden now. *"Bold oxlips and the crown imperial..."*
    —SHAKESPEARE,
    The Winter's Tale, Act IV.

28

This is Floralia, the ancient Roman festival for the goddess of blossoms and youth. It was traditional to pluck flowering hawthorne boughs on this day.

Prepare for May Eve mischief! Hang garlic and rowan leaves round the baby's cradle to keep the wee folk away.

29

"If you find an ash leaf or a four-leaved clover, You'll see your true love ere the day be over."

Girls wishing to know who will be their husbands must place a two-leaved clover in their shoes, reciting,
*"A clover of two, a clover of two,
Put it in your right shoe.
The first young man you meet,
In field or lane or street,
You'll have him or one of his name."*

MAY EVE

30

May Eve is a traditional night to burn the Beltane (bright fire).

Chaucer described Maying: *"fourth goth al the Court, both most and lest, to fetch the flouis fresh and braunch and blome."*

"It has been said of a hundred maids who go to the wood on May Eve, scarcely a third of them return home undefiled."
    —PHILIP STUBBES, 1586

ABOVE: *wild geranium.*

MAY

1

May Day is the Celtic festival of summer's beginning. It is sometimes still called Bal'tein Day in country places. Baal is the Gaelic word for globe. Beltane fires were lit for the return of the sun.

Today is the day to hang bunches of herbs and flowers on the door of friends and loved ones for good luck. Some of the customary greenery was sweet woodruff, pennyroyal, hawthorne, birch, and rowan. Blackthorn was bad luck.

Flowers were gathered on May Day to honor the Roman Goddess Flora (and adorn the churches and wells as late as 1504, according the list of Parish expenses in Coate's *History of Reading.*)

"Maie poole bound rounde about with flowers and hearbes and strings from top to bottom."
—16th-century description

The Puritans in America and Britain tried to discourage May Poles, but the people so loved them, they persisted to this day.
—*Herbal Almanac*

Just think, all of this celebration was for the universal joy at the world's greening once more!

2

The May Lady was a figure dressed and placed upon the table with wine and food set before her. She was often garlanded with hawthorne, the herb of May.

CROSS DAY *or* ROOD DAY

3

Feast of finding the Holy Cross.

4

"The eating of Sage in the Month of May, with Butter, Parsley, and some Salt is very commendable to the Body; as also sage-ale made with it, is good for Teeming women, such as are subject to miscarry through too much moisture or slipperyness of their Wombs. At all times be sure you wash your Sage, for fear that Toads should leave some Venom on the leaves, the danger whereof is on record; therefore it is good to plant Rue among your sage; and then they will not come near it."
—WILLIAM COLES,
Adam in Eden. 1657

5

Move your potted bay tree outside today.

6

MAY SALADS: *"To make a sallet of all kings of Herbs. Take your Herbs (as the tops of Sage, Mint, Lettuce, Violets, Marigolds, Spinach, etcetera) and pick them very fine in fair water; and wash your flowers by themselves and swing them in a strainer. Then mingle them in a dish with cucumbers and Lemons pared and sliced; scrape thereon sugar and put in Vinegar and oil. Spread your Flowers on top of the Sallet, and take Eggs boiled hard and lay them about the Dish."*
—THOMAS JENNER,
A Book of Fruits and Flowers. 1653

OPPOSITE: *violets, wild geranium and chamomile;* ABOVE: *sage.*

MAY

7

Wood Sorrel now in bloom: "All sorrel sauces is best, not only in virtue, but also in the pleasantest of taste."
—JOHN GERARD, *Herbal.* 1633

8

This is the day for Floral Dance and Robin Hood May Games. Morris Dancing is often done on this day. These were ten men who danced the Maid Marian dance with a hobby horse, twenty scarves and a Fool of May. The origins of the Morris dances are Spanish and the name comes from "Moorish". Maid Marian or the Queen of the May was sometimes also called Malykn or May Marian and she always carried a nosegay of flowers and sweet herbs. She wore a golden crown, and red gilliflowers (carnations) were her emblems of summer.

A 15th-century manuscript describes on this day how *"windows, dores and lights were garlanded against fairie, elves and sprites."*

9

Violets are in bloom. Add them to your salads today.

10

Ascension Day, Holy Thursday, Rogationtide. Today is the traditional day for a picnic! It is the day for blessing the fruits of the earth. *"In Country parishes it was the custom for the priest to go round the bounds of the parish and ask God for blessing of the fruits of the earth. It also kept fresh to each generation where the boundaries fell. A long pole was carried, clothed in flowers and herbs."*
—WITHER, 1635

11

Sweet woodruff is in bloom. Make your May wine.

This is the Roman festival of Lemuria, the festival of departed souls. Black beans and buckthorn were chewed to disperse lingering spirits.

ST. PANCRA'S DAY

12

St. Pancra is the patron saint of children. Plant a tiny herb garden for the children today. Include thyme, rosemary, marigolds, and chamomile and parsley (in honor of Peter Rabbit).

ABOVE: *sweet woodruff.*

MAY

13

May Day, Old Style

Lady's Mantle is in bloom now. Be sure to wash your girl child's face with the drop of dew which gathers in each leaf at dawn, and she will grow up fair. *"Our Lady's Mantle is an herb of green colour and groweth in moist meadows. In the night it closeth itself together like a purse, and the morning it is found full of dew."*
　　　　—WILLIAM TURNER, *Herbal.* 1568

16

Fairy changelings are often substituted for mortal children in May. Hang these herbs over the cradle to prevent this: rowan, rue, and dill.

14

Plant Hen and Chicks (Sempervivum) to keep lightning out of the garden.

17

Comfrey is now in bloom. *"The slimy substance of the root made into a posset of ale, are given to drink against the pain in the back, gotten by any violent motion (as wrestling or overmuch use of women) doth in four or five days perfectly cure the same, although the involuntary flowing of seed in men may be gotten thereby."*
　　　　—JOHN GERARD, *Herbal.* 1633

15

Take the first harvest of lemon balm.

18

This is often Whitsuntide. This day is the customary day for well-dressing. Wells and springs are decorated with flowers and sweet herbs to insure good water for the next year.

ABOVE: *germander* (15) and *rue* (16).

MAY

19

Sometimes this is Trinity Sunday. It is customary for a garland of herbs and flowers to be worn by a maiden who is kissed three times (in honor of the trinity) by a bachelor of another parish. Then there is a feast in her house.

20

It is bad luck to marry in May and bad luck to marry in a green dress.

21

The sun enters the house of Gemini today. Hands are ruled by the sign of Gemini, so all palm readers should be Geminis. Herbs to promote the well-being of those born under Gemini are mulberry leaves against the biting of serpents, parsley against the dangers that come to them that have lethargy, southern-wood drives away venomous creatures and helps those whose hair has fallen, and honey-suckle to ease the eyes. Valerian is singularly good for those that are short-winded. It is of special virtue against the plague.

22

Feverfew is in bloom today. Other folk names are featherfew and maydes weede. It was thought to strengthen the womb and entice the fairies to dance in your garden. *"So light and true that they shake no dew, From featherfew..."*
—NORA HOPPER

23

Celandine blooms today. A folk name is swallow wort. It was thought to improve eyesight. *"The juice of this herb is good to sharpen the sight, for it clearseth and consumeth away slimy things that cleave about the ball of the eye and hinder the sight."*
—JOHN GERARD, *Herbal.* 1633

24

May Cheeses are made this day. Nettle Cheese sounds interesting. *"As soon as cheese is drained from the brine, lay it upon fresh nettles to ripen. Renew nettles every few days and turn the cheese."*
—GERVASE MARKHAM, *The English Housewife.* 1683

ABOVE: *feverfew.*

MAY

25

Salad burnet is ready for the first harvest. The cool flavor is like cucumber — add it to the evening salad or make little burnet sandwiches.

26

St. Urban is the patron saint of vintner's. It was traditional to set up tables in the market-place *"strewn with greene leaves and sweete hearbes"* upon which an image of the bishop was placed.

27

The earliest strawberries are ripe. Crush new mint leaves with the strawberries now.

28

In May the tarragon leaves are curling up just like the little dragons from which it gets it name. Make a seafood salad with tarragon today.

29

Wear oak leaves to commemorate Charles II's escape in 1651 from the Parliamentarians; he hid in an oak tree.

30

Dandelions are in full bloom now. They make the traditional dandelion wine, and the leaves are diuretic. In fact, a folk name is Piss-a-bed.

31

Roman Saecular Games were per-formed for Pluto and Proserpine on this day. Celebrants wore crowns of bay.

ABOVE: *tarragon.*

JUNE

1

*"A dry May and a rainy June
Puts the Farmer's pipe in tune.
June damp and warm
Doth the farmer no harm."*

ST. ELMO'S DAY
2

St. Elmo is the patron saint of sailors. Parsley and violets are special herbs to prevent scurvy — they are both rich in vitamin C.

3

Take the first major harvest of the herbs. When the Flower Moon of June is between the last quarter and the new moon, it's the best time to harvest and weed the garden.

4

Roses are in bloom now. Rosa gallica is the old apothecary rose. It is the appropriate rose for the herb garden with its heady scent and flavorful oil.

5

This is the traditional day to shear sheep. Herbs to protect the fleece from insect damage are southernwood, lavender, mugwort, and tansy.

6

Lovage is glorious now. It is the symbol of everlasting devotion.

OPPOSITE: *strawberries and rue;* ABOVE: *parsley.*

JUNE

7

June is the luckiest time for weddings. A bridal bouquet should include a sprig of sage to insure domestic peace, good health and a long life; a sprig of lavender for undying love; jasmine for harmony; a sprig of marjoram, the gypsy herb of love; a sprig of borage for courage — always borage.

8

"If on the eighth of June it rain, that foretells a wet harvest, men sayen."
— Brand's *Popular Antiquities*

ST. COLUMBA'S DAY

9

This is the luckiest day of the year if it falls on a Thursday. St. Johnswort is St. Columba's herb too. It must be found accidentally and kept beneath the armpit (where St. Columba wore it) to ward off evil. This charm is recited when you pick the herb:

"Arm-pit package of Columba the kindly,
Unsought by me, unlooked for
I Shall not be carried away in my sleep
Neither shall I he pierced with iron.
Better the reward of its virtues
Than a herd of white cattle."

Ancient Roman Vestalia on this day was to implore blessings from the goddess Vesta for successful baking. Loaves decked with herbal and flowery wreaths were carried about.

10

This is a traditional day to rid the forest of undergrowth.

ST. BARNABAS DAY

11

Make the traditional Barnaby Garlands. On this day it is customary to deck churches and houses with garlands of roses and sweet woodruff, says John Gerard (1633). St. Barnabas was a peace-maker. He settled particularly tricky disputes.

12

If orange blossoms are included in the June bridal bouquet, know that they are the symbol of fecundity. Orange blossoms represented a pagan appeal to the orange tree spirit that the bride bear many children.

ABOVE: *borage* (7) and *St. Johnswort* (12).

JUNE

13

The herb garden is never more beautiful than in mid-June. Take a day to just enjoy it. Do no weeding, no harvesting and no coddling of the herbs — just observe their beauty and enjoy the sweet scents.

14

Honeysuckle is in bloom. In addition to its heavenly scent along country roads at dusk, it was useful as a tea to soothe a sore throat or to bathe an aching head. Be wary of it in the garden. *"...although it be very sweete, yet I not bring it into my garden but let it nest in his own place."*
—JOHN PARKINSON, 1629

15

Mullein stalks are blooming yellow now. The fuzzy green leaves were used to diaper babies and smoked to relieve coughs. The Saxons believed a leaf in one's pocket would keep away robbers and wild beasts — all the while making one's thoughts turn to romance.

16

Herb Robert (wild geranium) is now in full bloom. To wantonly destroy Herb Robert (adder's tongue, death-come-quickly) is to court snakebite or worse. Also it is called Poor Robert, Robin Hood, Robin-in-the-Hedge because it is under the protection of the household goblin Robin Goodfellow or Puck, and like him, it will help, especially in staunching wounds.

17

Lady's Bedstraw is now in bloom.
"The decoction of the herb called Lady's Bed-straw, being yet warm, is of admirable use to bathe the feet of Travellers."
—WILLIAM COLES, *Adam in Eden.* 1657

18

Elder flowers are out now. *"If your face be troubled with heat, take Elder-flowers, Plantain, white Daisy root and Herb Robert and put into running water and wash your face therewith at night and in the morning."*
—HANNAH WOOLLEY,
The Gentlewoman's Companion. 1675

ABOVE: *wild geranium.*

JUNE

19

Strawberries are now in full fruiting. *"The water of strawberries distilled is a sovereign remedy and cordial in the palpitations of the heart, that is panting and beating thereof."*
—WILLIAM COLES, *Adam in Eden.* 1657

20

Now is the time for earnest weeding! *"Thus I have limmed out a Garden to our Country House-wifes, and given them Rules for common herbs...The skill and pains of weeding the Garden with weeding knives or fingers, I refer to themselves, and their maids, willing them to take the opportunity of a shower of rain; withal, I advise the Mistress either to be present her self, or to teach her maids to know herbs from weeds."*
—WILLIAM LAWSON,
The Countrie Housewife's Garden. 1617

MIDSUMMER'S EVE

21

Eve of the Feast of St. John the Baptist.

"The pagan rites of this festival at the summer solstice may be considered as a counterpart of those used at the winter solstice at Yule-tide."
—BRAND'S *Antiquities*

On this night it is customary to build huge bonfires and make vows and sacrifices for the fruitfulness of the earth. The fires were built to entice the sun back from its shortening days.

Mugwort worn in one's shoe will cause one to be carried about the country-side on the back of a white horse until dawn when the horse will disappear and leave the rider stranded.

MIDSUMMER

22

The longest day of the year and the day the sun enters the House of Cancer.

Herbs for the special well-being of those born under the sign of Cancer are lemon balm to be merry, betony to cleanse, violets to dry up watery humours, daisies to give great ease to sore limbs and hyssop to strengthen all parts of the body.

23

The roses are still glorious.

*"For us the rose from year to year
    renews in abundance
The yellow stamens of its crimson flower,
Far and away the best of all in power
    and fragrance,
It well deserves its name,
'The Flower of Flowers.'"*
—WALAHFRID STRABO, *Hortulus.* 1510

24

Orange mint is abundant now. Make a merry-making summer punch from the recipe of an old Virginia herb woman of the Blue Ridge Mountains.

1 quart of chopped orange mint
3 *or* 4 bergamot flowers
2–3 lemons juice and rind
3 tablespoons of sugar
1 pint chopped spearmint
1 gallon of boiling water

MODE: Place herbs and lemon in enamel pot. Pour half the water over it. Steep 10–15 minutes. Strain. Add sugar and remaining water which is cooled. Makes 12 cups.

ABOVE: *lemon balm.*

JUNE

25

Dry petals now for colorful pot pourri next winter. Gather rose petals, calendula, larkspur, delphinium, geranium and clove pinks. Spread them out in a dark warm spot until they are chip dry.

26

Fairies are particularly active between Midsummer and St. Peter's Day, June 29.

Look for fairies dancing near the thyme under the moon in June. They like to leave their babies asleep in the tiny thyme blossom cradles. If you do see a fairy, never tell anyone — it will bring bad luck.

27

This is an old way to bind a fairy to you. Now is the best time of year.

"An excellent way to get a Fairy. First get a broad square crystal in length and breadth three inches, and lay it in the blood of a white hen three Wednesdays or three Fridays. Then take it out and wash it with Holy Water and fumigate it. Then take three hazel rods of a year's growth, peel them fair and white, and write the fairy's name (which you shall call three times) on every stick being made one side flat; Then bury them under some hill wheras you suppose fairies haunt. The Wednesday before you call her, and the Friday following call her three times at eight or three or ten of the clock. But when you call, be in Clean Life and turn thy face towards East, and when you have her, bind her in theat crystal."
    —ELIAS ASHMOLE'S *Manuscript,*
    late 17th century

28

Vervain *(Verbena communis)* blooms purple now. If you look through it into the firelight, you may see your future.

ST. PETER'S DAY / RUSH-BEARING DAY

29

This is the day to ceremoniously strew fresh rushes upon the floor. Rush carts were often the lavishly decorated focus of a procession.
"Good Day to you, you merry men all.
Come listen to our rhyme.
For we would have you not forget
This is Midsummer time.
So bring your rushes, bring your garlands,
Roses, John's Wort, Vervain, too.
Now is time for our rejoicing.
Come along Christians, come along do."
    —18th-century song

30

"Best time to make hay is a week after Midsummer when honeysuckles have lost their flowers."
    —GERVASE MARKHAM,
    The English Husbandman. 1633

ABOVE: *vervain* (28) *and hyssop* (30).

JULY

1

"In this month of July, eschew all wanton bed-sports, and of all things forbear lettuce."
—GERVASE MARKHAM,
The English Husbandman. 1633

2

Haymaking continues. *"Marsh woundwort or Husbandman's woundwort is good aginst wounds sustained in Haymaking."*
—JOHN GERARD, *Herbal.* 1633

3

Dog Days begin. Sirius, the dog star, is in ascent. It was once forbidden to take a physic of medicinal herbs on this day.

4

Midsummer's Eve, Old Style

"Maids slip 'Midsummer men' (slips of orphine) in chinks in the joists; one for the maid and one for the lover. If they incline together there would be love; recline, aversion."
—JOHN AUBREY,
Remains of Gentilism. 1688

5

Midsummer, Old Style

Beware of being led by Robin Goodfellow on this day! Wear a sprig of rue.

"There's rue for you; and here's some for me; we may call it herb of grace o'Sundays; O, you must wear your rue with a difference."
—SHAKESPEARE,
Hamlet, Act IV, Ophelia

6

"If a rabbit be killed in haymaking, fit it up for supper with Lettuce, Spynach, Parsley, Winter Savory and Sweet Marjoram."
—*The New Book of Cookery.* 1615

OPPOSITE: *dandelion, carnation, golden thyme and mint;* ABOVE: *rue.*

JULY

7

Herb Bennet (or Wood Avens) beginning to seed. *"Use it to rid one of summer spots."*
—WILLIAM TURNER, *Herbal.* 1568

10

Yarrow is in full bloom now. *"This plant Achillea is thought to be the very same wherewith Achilles cured the wounds of his souldiers."*
—JOHN GERARD, *Herbal.* 1633

8

Lilies begin to bloom now. *"Now the lily, and ah!...what lines can my simple Muse, lean and meagre as she is, find to praise the shining lily? If a snake...plants with deadly tongue its parcel Of venom in you...then crush lilies with a weighty pestle and drink the juice in wine... Then indeed you will learn for yourself the wonderful power this antidote has."*
—WALAHFRID STRABO, *Hortulus.* 1510

11

Sweet Marjoram is in flower today.
"A pleasant Mead of Sir William Paston': is to a Gallon of water a quart of honey, about ten sprigs of Sweet-Marjoram half so many tops of Bays. Boil these very well together, and when it is cold, bottle up. It will be ten days before it is ready to drink."
—*The Closet of Sir Kenelm Digby Opened* 1669

9

"Radishes and southernwood burned and made into powder anoint a bald place to remedy baldness of the head."
—EDWARD POTTER's *Phisicke Book.* 1610

12

Fennel is often setting seed by now.
"Fennel is for flatterers" is the old English saying. The Italian phrase "Dare Finocchio" (to give fennel) actually means "to flatter." This symbolism was such common knowledge in William Shakespeare's time that in Hamlet when Ophelia offered fennel to her brother, the audience immediately understood it was to warn him of flatterer's treachery.

ABOVE: *yarrow.*

JULY

13

This is an unlucky day to marry.

14

Water herb gardens only in the very driest of conditions (such as mid-July so often brings). Water herbs deeply and slowly to encourage tender new roots to grow downward rather than spread out to the surface where they will dry out quickly.

ST. SWITHIN'S DAY

15

All apples growing at this time will ripen and come to maturity.

Roman Rosalia, the feast of roses, ended on this day. The rose is sacred to Venus, goddess of love.

16

The waysides are starred with wild daisies now. *"The Daisies doe mitigate all kinde of paines, but especially of the joints."*
—JOHN GERARD, *Herbal.* 1633

17

Basil, the Queen of High Summer, is about to burst into bloom. In India it a sacred plant. Dioscorides, a 6th-century Greek garden writer, cautions that eating too much basil *"dulls the eyesight."* Basil leaves are given as a token of love. *"...it receives fresh life from being touched by a fair lady."*
—THOMAS TUSSER, 1573

18

The herb garden is lush with chives. Their lineage is over 3,000 years old (in our recorded history). This was pictured on ancient Egyptian monuments. King Oberon's elfin troupe puffed on tiny pipes made of hollow chive leaves, Romanian gypsies used chive stems to tell fortunes.

ABOVE: *basil* (15) and *violets* (16).

JULY

19

Wormwood is coming to seed. *"While wormwood hath seed, get a handful or twain. To save against March, to make fleas refrain where Chamber is swept — and wormwood is strown no flea, for his life, dare abide to be known."*
—THOMAS TUSSER, *Five Hundred Points of Good Husbandry.* 1573

FEAST *of* ST. WILGEFORTIUS
20

St. Wilgefortius was invoked by women who wished to unencumber themselves of troublesome husbands or importunate suitors. Picking parsley just at dawn and wishing aloud for release will do the same.

21

"July to whom the Dog Star in her train, St. James gives oysters and St. Swithin rain."
—BRAND'S *Antiquities*

Except for luck (or if St. Swithin directs some your way), it rarely rains this time of year; remember to water your newly-established perennial herbs as well as the annuals.

FEAST *of* ST. MARY MAGDALENE
22

St. Mary Magdalene is the patron saint of penitents or reformed prostitutes. Rue is the herb of penitents.
"Here is a shadowed grove which takes its color From the miniature forest of glaucous rue... Touch it but gently and it yields a heavy Fragrance. Many a healing power it has..."
—WALAHFRID STRABO, *Hortulus.* 1510

23

The sun enters the House of Leo. Herbs especially for the well-being of those born under this sign are Angelica to comfort the heart, Bay to protect from witch or devil, or thunder or lightening, Borage to expel melancholy, St. Johnswort for magic and to remove warts, and Marigolds to comfort the spirit.

Panathenaea, the ancient Greek festival to honor Athena was held once every five years at this time for six days. This was the last day, when the statue of Athena was adorned with flowers and sweet herbs.

ST. BRIDGET'S DAY
24

St. Bridget is the patron saint of Ireland and was a goddess of the Celtic Irish. A special little cake called Bairnbreac is made of barley and eaten in her honor on this day.

ABOVE: *marigold.*

JULY

25
ST. JAMES DAY / ST. CHRISTOPHER DAY

This is an auspicious day to begin a journey because it is the feast day of two traveling saints. It is also a day to bless the new apples. *"Benedicto Pomorum in Die Sancti Jacobi."*
—MANVALE, *ad Usum Sarum.* 1555

Salacia, Neptune's wife, was honored on this Roman holiday. Olive boughs were erected in arbors to encourage an abundance of water during the dry time of year.

26
FEAST *of* ST. ANNE

St. Anne is the patron saint of housewives. Meadowsweet or Queen of the Meadow is the herb dedicated to her.

"The leaves and flowerings far excell all other strewing herbs, for to deck up houses, to strew in chambers, halls, and banquetting houses in the summer time; for the smell thereof makes the heart merry."
—JOHN GERARD, *Herbal.* 1633

27

This may be Mace Monday. It is traditional to stick a cabbage on a pole and carry it like a mace. It is also traditional to eat beans on this day.

28

Fill the house with all the sweet herbs now in their glory.

"Come, sweetheart, come,
Dear as my heart to me
Come to the room
I have made for thee...
Flowers for thee to tread,
Green herbs, sweet scented."
—10th-century song

29

It is time for an herbal iced tea!

"The Muse's friend, tea does our fancy aid,
Repress those vapours which the head invade,
And keep that palace of the soul serene."
—EDMUND WALLER

30
Self-sown seedlings of borage will often be blooming now. The bright blue blossoms nod cheerfully. Borage is the medieval symbol of courage and was often a motif in embroidery.

31
Herbs seem to be in a determined growth spurt. It is a good time to take cuttings of rosemary, lavender, tarragon and scented geraniums. Keep them in the shade until new roots are established.

ABOVE: *rosemary.*

AUGUST

I

This is the festival of the beginning of harvest. It is one of the four great druid festivals of the year. "Gul" is the Gaelic word for wheel or circle or re-occurrence. This is also the festival of the Celtic God Lugh Lightborn, and it is a good time to divine the future. Wheat cakes of the first harvest were made and seasoned with dill at this time in honor of the mother aspect of the earth goddess.

2

Feverfew is now in bloom.

"Good against summer headaches to inhale crushed feverfew blossoms, Dried and taken with honey or sweet wine good for those as be melancholic, sad, pensive or without speech."
—JOHN GERARD, *Herbal.* 1633

3

Watch for summer snakes. Herbalist William Turner insisted that burning southernwood branches would drive away snakes.

4

Sunflowers are in full bloom now. The sunflower is the symbol of constancy as its face follows the path of the sun.

"Oh, the heart that has truly loved never forgets,
But as truly loves on to the close,
As the sunflower turns on her god, when he sets,
The same look which she turned when he rose!"
—THOMAS MOORE

5

Be wary of drinking too many icy drinks when the weather is scorching. *"Harvest Daisy decoction cures all Diseases that are occasioned by excessive drinking of cold beer when the body is hot."*
—JOHN PECHEY, *The Compleat Herbal of Physical Plants.* 1694

6

Benne seeds ripen now. Sesame *(Sesamum orientale)* is the West African plant of good luck. Just growing the little plant in the garden is sure to bring good fortune to the whole family. It is called benne in South Carolina where it was first brought by slaves.

OPPOSITE: *sage, black-eyed susan and fern;* ABOVE: *fewerfew.*

AUGUST

7

Insects intrude upon us in August! Wear oil of citronella dabbed behind each ear to discourage gnats and mosquitoes. It is made from lemon balm. Wear a string of tonka beans or a little patchouli for the same purpose.

8

It is a good day to make herb vinegars. Simply steep a cup of fresh herb leaves of almost any sort in a pint of white wine vinegar for a month.

9

If there is a drought now, try burning fern bracken. It is said to cause rain.

10

ST. LAWRENCE'S DAY

St. Lawrence is the patron saint of cooks. Hang a little wreath of sage, thyme, rosemary, and marjoram to honor him.

11

Lammas Eve, Old Style

Lammas is an uncanny and spirit-haunting time. Rowan crosses were fastened above doors and windows. This must be secretly done or the charm would be broken.

12

Lammas Day, Old Style

There was often a great fair at this time, and it is an ancient custom for unmarried couples to pledge loyalty and live together until the next Lammas Fair. This was called "handfasting." If they were well-pleased with their mates at the next fair, they married. If not, they parted honorably. Sage is the herb of domestic peace and tranquillity. Hang a sprig in the house!

ABOVE: *lemon balm* (7) and *cowslips* (9).

AUGUST

FEAST of ST. CASSIAN

13 St. Cassian is the patron saint of school teachers. Mint and lavender are the herbs to stimulate the brain and make learning easier. Every teacher should have a pot of mint and a bowl of dried lavender flowers on the desk.

This is also the ancient Greek festival of Hecate, the moon goddess. She was invoked to protect the heavily laden vines and gardens from storms until the harvest was reaped. The Roman Catholic Church continued the festival on August 15 with the Assumption of the Virgin Mary.

14

Harvest flowers are now in bloom, and it is unlucky to pick them before the harvest is over. They are Harvest Bells, Harvest Daisies, Harvest Lilies (bindweed) and Harebells (or Fairy Caps or Fairy Ringers).

ASSUMPTION of the VIRGIN MARY

15 It was customary on this day to ask blessings upon herbs, plants, roots, and fruits.

For the Great St. Mary's Feast of Harvest: (in Scotland) To make the traditional Mary's Bannock, pluck ears of new corn (grain), dry them in the sun, grind with stones, make into a cake and toast with magical rowan sticks. A piece of bannock must be eaten by each member of the family in order of ages and all must then walk clockwise around the fire.

ST. ROCH'S DAY

16 St. Roch was a 10th-century plague doctor.

On this day take special precautions against contagious disease. Not this! *"For the Pestilence, Take of Sage, Yarrow and Tansy and Feverfew, — each a handful and then bruise them well. Then let the sick party make water in the herbs; then strain them and give it to the sick to drink."*
—GERVASE MARKHAM,
The English Husbandman. 1633

17

This is time to gather herb seeds for next year's planting.

"Seeds must be gathered in fair weather, at the wane of the moon and kept in boxes of wood."
—GERVASE MARKHAM,
The English Housewife. 1683

ST. HELEN'S DAY

18 St. Helen was invoked to protect from fire, lightning and tempest. *"Also protective against lightning and useful to cure burns is the succulent leaved Houseleek or Senngreen, once carefully cultured on roofs and still found there. Old writers call it Jupiter's Beard."*
—WILLIAM BULLEIN,
Book of Simples. 1562

The Ancient Roman country Vinalia festival was held for Venus and Minerva. Kitchen gardeners went on holiday. Minerva protects the olive yard and Venus the garden.

ABOVE: *lavendar.*

AUGUST

19

"For lethargy or extreme drowsiness provoked by heat,...white wine and Hyssop water."
—GERVASE MARKHAM,
The English Housewife. 1683

20

Bright yellow tansy buttons are ripe for harvesting in the wayside. Hang them in bunches to keep insects out of the room now, and when they are dried they will remain colorful all winter.

21

Wild Tansy is also called Silverweed or Traveler's Ease.

"It is certain that your carriers wear the leaves of silverweed in their shoes, which keeps them cool and prevents a too immoderate sweating of the feet which causes a soreness in them."
—DEERING, *Catalogus Stirpium.* 1738

22

"Sage leaves, yarrow and ale are recommended for a gnawing at a heart, for the benefit of poor poets and disappointed authors."
—WEDSECNARF,
17th century

23

The sun enters the house of Virgo today. Herbs especially for the well-being of those born under the sign of Virgo are fennel to promote a healthy glow, stay the hiccoughs and make more lean those too fat. Savory will take away the sting of rebuke, chamomile to prevent weariness and Lavender for good use in relieving griefs and pains of the head.

Virgo was known in ancient Greece as Dore or Virgo Cereres, the wheat-bearing maiden.

FEAST *of* ST. BARTHOLOMEW
24

The great St. Bartholomew's Fair was held in London on this day. Because the taverns could not supply enough ale, certain houses were given license to sell spirits. Green oak branches were hung above their doors — bough houses.

St. Bartholomew is the patron saint of tanners, leatherworkers, and bookbinders. A sprig of rue in each book is said to prevent silverfish.

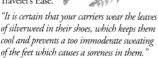

ABOVE: *tansy* (21) and *hyssop* (22).

AUGUST

25

"*Sap from the ash tree is given to children this time of year in the Shetland Islands because it was thought to be a powerful astringent and it possessed the property of resisting attacks of witches, fairies and other imps of the darkness.*"
—Bell and Dadly, *Choice Notes from "Notes and Queries" Folklore.* 1859

26

If a summer thunder storm threatens on this day recall: "*Many also to weare vervein against blasts; and when they gather it for this purpose, firste they crosse the herbe with their hand, and then bless it with a charm.*"
—13th-century manuscript

27

Wild poppies grow in among the corn rows this time of year. Staring too long at them is said to cause blindness. Poppies are symbol of the ancient Greek goddess Parthenos, the maiden.

Of the juice of poppies: "*...if a man takes too much, taketh a man's memory away, and killeth him.*"
—William Turner, *Herbal.* 1568

28
ST. AUGUSTINE'S DAY

St. Augustine is the patron saint of readers and booklovers. He had fallen away in his belief when his mother died and couldn't read or concentrate. One day he lay down beneath an oak tree in the shade and prayed for faith. A voice rang out to him in the shady bower, "*Take up and read,*" it said. From that day forth he was a reader and a true believer.

Keep a pressed oak leaf in your books to honor St. Augustine.

29

It's a good time to collect horehound to preserve for winter cough remedies. Horehound is a pretty little plant to grow in a place that is usually scraggly or bare. This is a recipe for old-fashioned Horehound Drops, "*Combine strong horehound tea with two cups of sugar and a pinch of cream of tartar. Cook the mixture over low heat until a drop will become hard in a glass of cold water. Pour the mixture in a buttered shallow plate and score into little squares when half-hardened. When completely cooled, break into pieces and store in a cool, dry place.*"

30

According to tradition this was the day the dove returned to the ark bearing an olive branch, the symbol of peace in the world.

31

Warts were charmed away by making a cross over the wart with elder sticks.

Above: *savory.*

SEPTEMBER

1

St. Giles is the patron saint of the physically handicapped.

"This month thou mayest Physicke take
And Bleed and bathe for thy health's sake
Eat figs, and grapes and spicery
For to refresh thy members dry"
—NEVE'S *Almanack.* 1633

2

Oliver Cromwell died on this day in 1658. Mrs. Cromwell's recipe for Green Sauce for a Hen called for sorrel and vinegar poured over the roasting bird.

3

Early autumn seems to be the best time to plant garlic. Take a firm plump garlic bulb and divide it into cloves. Plant them two inches deep and five inches apart.

4

"September blow soft till Fruit be in Loft."

Thomas Tusser's advice for September is: *"Set herbes some more for winter store, Sow seeds for pot, for flowers not."*
—THOMAS TUSSER, *'Five Hundred Points of Good Husbandry.* 1573

5

The Hock Carts (harvest carts) bring home the last harvest from the field. It was traditional to deck them with garlands of herbs and oak leaves.

6

This is the traditional time to put new straw in straw mattresses. It was a good idea to include a little pennyroyal to keep away fleas. "Lady in the Straw" was an old-fashioned name for a woman about to give birth.

OPPOSITE: *Michaelmas daisy, columbine and marigold;* ABOVE: *wood sorrel.*

SEPTEMBER

7

Furmenty was an old dish made of the new wheat.

"Wife, sometime this weeke if all thing go cleare,
an ende of wheat sowing we make for this yeare,
Remember you therefore though I do it not
The Seede Cake, the Pasties, and Furmenty pot."
—THOMAS TUSSER, 1557

8 FEAST *of the* NATIVITY *of the* BLESSED VIRGIN MARY

Some of the herbs dedicated to the Virgin are Our Lady's Delight (violets), Lavender, Madonna Lily, Marigold, Mary's Eyes (Forget-Me-Not), Mary's Hands (potentilla), Mary's Slippers (monkshood), Our Lady's Balsam (costmary), Our Lady's Basin (teasel), Our Lady's Bedstraw, Our Lady's Eardrops (fuchia), Our Lady's Hair (maidenshair fern), Lady's Mantle, Our Lady's Needle (wormwood), Our Lady's Shoes (columbine), Rosemary, Our Lady of the Meadow (spirea), Mary's Tears (star of Bethlehem), Thyme, Virgin Flower (periwinkle).

9

Hedgerow trees are now in bloom. Mountain ash (wicken, witchbeam, witty) is the most powerful of all plants against evil and witchcraft. The red-orange berries make a tart jelly to serve with meat or cheese. *"Rowen tree and red thread hold witches in all dread."*

10

Rose hips are ripe. Collect them for a fine winter tea rich in vitamin C.

11

Hops picking begins now. Dried hops in a pillow ensure a good night's sleep and sweet dreams.

12

This month is the effectual time for taking medicine.

"GOOD FOR THE HEART: *Saffron, borage, laughing joy, musk, cloves, nutmegs, galingale, the red rose, the violet and mace.*
EVIL FOR THE HEART: *Beans, peas, leeks, garlic, onions, heaviness, anger, dread, too much business travel, to drink cold water, evil tidings."*
—*Calendar of Shepheardes*, 1604

ABOVE: *borage* (7) and *catnip* (11).

SEPTEMBER

HOLY ROOD DAY
13

Holy Rood Day is the beginning of the rutting season. Hazelnuts collected upon this day have magic properties (especially two nuts in one stalk will cure a tooth ache, rheumatism or spells of witches). To pick hazelnuts unripe is extremely unlucky.

The Anglo-Saxon word "rood" means "cross." In AD 615 the Emperor Heraclius recovered a large piece of the Holy Cross from the infidels.

14

This is the traditional time for Harvest Fairs. Everyone came to the fair towns and stayed at inns on the direct road (or arms) outside of town. That is why so many inns have the name "Arms" attached, as in Boult's Arms or Kings Arms.

15

It is time to harvest artemisia, wormwood, and southernwood for moth protection. *"The branches and leaves laid amongst cloathes keepeth them from moths, whereupon it hath beene called of some Moth-weed, or Mothwort. The floures stand on the tops of the stalkes, joyned together in tufts...which being gathered before they be ripe or withered, remaine beautiful long time after."*
—John Gerard, *Herbal.* 1597 edition

ST. NINIAN'S DAY
16

St. Ninian's plant symbol is southernwood, called "apple-ringie" in Scotland. Southernwood was used by the Romans in spells against impotence. Another folk name is Lad's Love. It was presented by bachelors to the girl of their choice. Southernwood is also used to take away pimples when mixed with barley meal for a facial mask.

17

Pears are now ripe. *"Fragrant and perfectly ripened pears generate cold blood and are therefore suited to those with hot temperaments, in the heat and in southern regions. They are salubrious for people with weak stomachs, but harmful to the production of bile. The harm can be remedied by chewing cloves of garlic after the meal."*
—*Tacuinum Sanitatis in Medicina* (translated in *The Four Seasons of the House of Cerruti*), 14th century

18

If you unwisely eat unripe fruit, nettle seed tea will cure the ill effects.

Above: *violets.*

SEPTEMBER

19

It was traditional for maidens to gather crab apples from the hedgerows today. It is also traditional to roast a goose today. An old rental fee was a goose on Michaelmas.

20

Make lavender caps against the onset of winter. *"I judge that the flowers of lavender, quilted into a cap and daily worn, are good for all diseases of the head that come of a cold cause, and that they comfort the brain very well, namely, if it have any distemperature that cometh of moistness."*
—WILLIAM TURNER, *Herbal.* 1568

ST. MATHEW'S DAY
21

St. Mathew is the patron saint of bankers, tax collectors and others in finance. Make a dried bouquet of the money plant (lunaria) in his honor today.

"St. Mathew's Day bright and clear, Brings good wine in next year."

22

Harvest fruits at the waning moon.

23

The sun enters the house of Libra today. Herbs to promote the well-being of those born under the sign of Libra are pennyroyal to cool, moneywort to heal wounds exceedingly, mugwort to ease pains in the neck, peach leaves to procure rest and sleep (also to marvelously cause hair to grow again upon bald places) and tansy, the best companion for women, their lovers excepted.

24

In ancient Greece the Greater Eleusinian Mysteries began today. They lasted nine days to celebrate the great goddesses. Matrons of Athens carried coffers of mysterious things, including herbs (marjoram), wheat and barley to the temple of Eleusis.

ABOVE: *lovage.*

SEPTEMBER

25

Pick blackberries today before the devil befouls them on old Michealmas. *"Leaves of the bramble (blackberry) boiled in water with honey and white wine make a most excellent lotion or washing water and will fasten the teeth."*
—JOHN GERARD, *Herbal.* 1633

26

Holy Rood Day, Old Style

Women and girls gathered wild carrots today by digging a triangular hole (St. Michael's shield) with a 3-pronged mattock or hoe. The carrots were tied with red thread and presented to male visitors on Michaelmas Day. Forked carrots were especially lucky.

ST. COSMOS DAY /
27
ST. DAMIAN'S DAY

St. Cosmos and St. Damian were doctors who practiced without charging fees. Now they are the patron saints of doctors and apothecaries.

28

Michaelmas Eve, Old Style

The Michaelmas lamb was killed this day. A blemish-free lamb was prepared to be cooked on Michaelmas over a fire of sacred oak, rowan and bramblewood.

29

Michaelmas, Old Style

St. Michael the Archangel was the greatest foe of Satan. He is the patron saint of knights, warriors and souls of the dead. The herb dedicated to him is the beautiful and sweet angelica.

Today was the greatest of the autumn festivals!

30

Michaelmas daisies, or wild asters bloom now. *"The Michael Daisy among dead weeds, Blooms for St. Michael's valorous deeds."*

ABOVE: *marigold.*

OCTOBER

1

This is the proper time of year to make sympathetic potions from the herbs to cure wounds. They were applied to the weapon which caused the wound. Rodolphus Goclous of Wittenburg advocated this method in 1608.

ST. SYLVESTER'S DAY

2

St. Sylvester is the protector of forests.

3

"Harvest Home, Harvest Home
We've ploughed, we've sowed,
We've reaped, we've mowed
And brought home every load."
—Traditional harvest song

ST. FRANCIS' DAY

4

This beloved saint was born into a wealthy family at Assisi in 1182. His exuberant youthful pranks landed him in prison, but he underwent a spiritual transformation, living in humility and poverty to the end of his days. He believed the earth was his mother and all living things were his brothers and sisters. A little herb garden dedicated to St. Francis should always include juniper, myrtle, angelica, nepeta and a fig tree.

5

Pineapple sage is often still blooming now in the herb garden. Hummingbirds are particularly attracted to the bright red blossoms.

ST. FAITH'S DAY

6

St. Faith was a virgin martyr, and on this day young girls can divine their future husbands by making a St. Faith cake with spring water and rosemary. They must cut the cake into nine pieces, pass it through the wedding ring of a woman married seven years, and then eat of the cake saying,
O Good St. Faith, be kind tonight
And bring to me my heart's delight
Let me my future husband view
And be my vision chaste and true."

OPPOSITE: *fig and borage;* ABOVE: *sweet woodruff.*

OCTOBER

7

Gather plums today. *"Plums are under Venus, and like women, some better and some worse."*
—Nicolas Culpeper, *Herbal.* 1653

8

The last crab apples are ripe now. Lambs-wool is a brew of ale, nutmeg, sugar and toasted crab apples. The name comes from the very old Celtic "Lamasaghel". Shakespeare (in Love's Labour's Lost) says it is the time of year *"When roasted crabs hiss in the bowl...."*
—Act V, Scene 2, Song sung by all

9

The last herb stalk in the garden after harvest harbors the spirit of the garden. It should be tied up with ribbon and hung in the kitchen.

10

This was the traditional day for Michaelmas Spring, or Indian Summer; one fine day before the cold sets in.

ST. LUKE'S DAY

11

On St. Luke's Day take marigold flowers, a sprig of marjoram, thyme and a little wormwood. Dry them before a fire, rub them to powder, then sift thro a fine piece of lawn. Simmer these with a small quantity of virgin honey in white vinegar over a slow fire. With this anoint your stomach, breast and lips lying down and repeat these words thrice,
"St. Luke, St. Luke, be kind to me,
In dreams let me my true love see."
If he approaches you with a smile in your dreams he will prove a loving husband. But if he be one who will forsake thy bed to wander after strange women, he will be rude to thee in your dream.
—*Mother Bunch's Closet Newly Broke Open* (an old chapbook)

12

Roman Fontinalia was the festival in which wells and springs were garlanded with herbs to honor the god Fons, son of Janus.

OCTOBER

13

Of ancient
herbal charms to
cure diseases, there are five rules:
1) The person to be healed must first believe.
2) The charmer and charmee must never use
the words "please" or "thank you." 3) If once
disclosed, the charm would lose its effective-
ness. 4) The charm must be passed from
mothers to daughters on dying lips. 5) Offer
of remumeration would break the charm.
     —*Choice Notes: Folklore.* 1859

14

"*Onion's skin very thin
Mild winter coming in
Onion's skin thick and tough
Coming winter cold and rough.*"

15

Ancient Roman festival of the October
Horse, the last harvest festival. The horse
symbolizes fertility and the corn spirit still
symbolized in the hobby horse garlanded
with flowers and herbs.

Purslane is still green in October. To strew
purslane round one's bed was a protection
from magic. It also fastened loose teeth.

16

"*There is no Herbe nor weede but God hath
gyven venture them to helpe man!*"
     —Dr. ANDREW BOORDE,
     Dyetary. 16th century

17

It is time to bring in the bay tree.
"*The Gods, that mortal beauty chase,
Still in a tree did end their race.
Apollo hunted Daphne so,
Only that she might laurel grow.
And Pan did after Syrinx speed,
Not as a nymph, but for a reed.*"
     —ANDREW MARVELL, *The Garden*

18

The luckiest day of the
year to choose a husband.

ABOVE: *basil* (13) and *purslane* (18).

OCTOBER

19

Thyme is its most beautiful in the garden now.
"O! And I was a damsel so fair,
But fairer I wished to appear,
So I washed me in milk,
and I dressed me in silk,
And put the sweet thyme in my hair."
—An old Devonshire song

20

Pull up a stock of kale today. If clumps of dirt stick to the roots, it is good fortune.

ST. URSULA'S DAY
21

St. Ursula was the patron saint of virgins and girls' schools. This is Queen Elizabeth's (the virgin queen) receipt for wind: *"Take ginger, cinnamon, galingale, aniseseed, fennelseed, mace, nutmeg. Pound together with sugar. Use this before or after meat."*
—*Fairfax Household Book.* 17th century

22

It is the traditional time for young girls to go out and pull three oat stalks with their eyes closed. If the third stalk lacks a "top pickle" (the grain at the top), the girl will come to her marriage bed anything but a maid.

23

The sun enters the house of Scorpio today. Herbs especially for the well-being for those born under Scorpio are basil to protect from the sting of a bee and to inspire amorous thoughts, plantain to ease the pain of the head and help frantic persons very much, chamomile to take away weariness, and lavender which is especially good for all griefs and pains of the head.

24

The cure for lethargy is to sniff horseradish water vigorously up the nose!

ABOVE: *chamomile.*

OCTOBER

ST. CRISPIN'S DAY
25

St. Crispin is the patron saint of shoemakers and cobblers. *"The 25th of October, cursed be the cobbler that goes to bed sober."*

26

Gather sloes for wine or jelly. This is a sure remedy for diarrhea.
"By the end of October, go gather up sloes
Have thou in a readiness plenty of those.
And keep them in bedstraw, or still on the bough
to stay both the flux of thyself and thy cow."
—THOMAS TUSSER, 1573

27

A country cure for ringworm in children was a poultice of rotten apples, treacle, Borage, Soapwort, Wormwood and Rue.

ST. SIMON'S / ST. JUDE'S DAY
28

St. Simon is the patron saint of woodcutters and St. Jude is the patron saint of lost causes. Peel an apple in one piece and throw it over your left shoulder while reciting the following rhyme.
"St. Simon and St. Jude, on you I intrude.
By this paring I hold to discover
Without any delay, to tell me this day
The first letter of my own true love."
The paring will land in the correct initial. If the paring breaks, you won't marry at all.

29

Make a corn dollie to preside over your home for the winter. She was traditionally made with the last stalks from the harvest garden, and she has many folk names: Countryman's Favor, Earth Mother, Corn Baby, Ivy Girl and Welsh Border Fan. We make ours from straw, and she carries a basket of lavender for purity, rosemary for remembrance, bay for triumph, tansy for immortality, sage for domestic happiness and thyme to help us keep our minds open to the old magic.

30

According to the book *Festyvall,* 1511, at this time of year good people bake seed cakes to give each member of the family and the poor saying, *"God have your soul, Beens and all."*

HALLOWEEN
31

Also called "All Hallow's Eve" or "Nutcrack Night." This is the last night of the old Celtic year. It is the night when country people believe mischief makers (devils, witches, aerial folk and fairies) are all about on baneful errands.

ABOVE: *rue.*

NOVEMBER

1

Samhain, the Celtic new year. On this day the harvest is traditionally blessed, and the deceased are especially remembered.

ALL SOUL'S DAY

2

This is All Soul's Day or Soulmas, the day on which special prayers are said for the souls of the departed. It is customary to place sprigs of rosemary on the graves of loved ones.

This is also the ancient Roman public occasion called Hilaria, so called because the people shouted for joy at the finding of the lost god Osiris. Fertile soil and herbs and spices were mixed and shaken into a figure representing this son of Isis.

3

Calendula or pot marigolds are often still blooming in the herb garden on this day. In many areas they bloom in each month of the year, hence their name "calendula" from the latin "calends," the first day of each month. One tradition says a person gathering calendula blossoms must be free from deadly sin and say three Pater Nosters and three Aves.

4

This is the traditional day to make ginger-bread with *"annisseed, ginger and cinnamon."*
—GERVASE MARKHAM,
The English Housewife. 1683

GUY FAWKES DAY

5

Guy Fawkes effigies are sometimes decked with herbs and carried through the village.

6

Parsley is often still green in the herb garden. Parsley tea is good for digestion, and it is a diuretic. One of parsley's folk names, like dandelions, is "Piss-a-bed." *"I knew a wench married in the afternoon as she went to the garden for a parsley to stuff a rabbit."*
—SHAKESPEARE, *Taming of the Shrew,*
Act IV, Scene 4, Biondello

OPPOSITE: *calendula, basil, juniper, rosemary and chervil;* ABOVE: *parsley.*

NOVEMBER

7

Grow a pot of chervil on the windowsill. It will thrive in a cool, drafty spot. It is said to make one youthful, *"cure the cold stomach of the aged"* and nibbling the leaves will drive away the hiccups. John Gerard wrote that chervil *"provoketh lust."*

8

The herb garden is finally at rest.
"The knot and border, and the rosemary gay
Do crave the like succour, for the dying away..."
—Thomas Tusser, 1573

9

Make an herb wreath with the wonderful dried bounty of the herb garden. Wreath-making is a noble and ancient practice. The circle is the symbol of immortality, and an herb wreath is symbolic of our growing seasons and their return each year.

10

Halloween, Old Style

Gather herb twigs for burning in the winter fire. Their smell is sweet!

The French festival of Reason and Liberty, represented by women wearing crowns of oak leaves.

MARTINMAS

11

Today is the festival of the beginning of winter.
"Winter, image of age, who like a great belly
Eats up the whole year's substance and heart
*   lessly*
Swallows the fruits of our unstinted labor."
—Walahfrid Strabo, *Hortulus.* 1510

12

Since grazing is becoming scanty, this is the traditional time for slaughtering pigs, sheep and cattle for winter meat. Sausage is made now. Season it with nutmeg, cloves, mace, sweet marjoram, thyme and pennyroyal according to *The Closet of Sir Kenelm Digby Opened 1669.*

ABOVE: *tansy.*

NOVEMBER

13

This is the traditional time to gather the last tansy to drive away insects and cure inflammations of the mouth, according to Nicolas Culpeper in his *Herbal* of 1653.

14

Lay in the winter firewood.
"Beechwood fires burn bright and clear
If logs be kept a year
Oaken logs if dry and old
Keep away the winter's cold
Chestnut's only good they say
If for years 'tis laid away
But ash-wood green or ash-wood brown
Are fit for a King with a golden crown."

15

Purslane may still be green in protected places. *"Purslane extynct the ardor of lassyvyousnes and doth mytygate great heate in all inwarde partes of man."*
    —Dr. Andrew Boorde,
    Dyetary. 16th century

16

A country cure for hoarseness is to rub the soles of the feet with garlic and lard. Radish juice is another cure for hoarseness.

17

Although ivy is harmful if eaten, it was used by herbalists to cure aches and pains. Ivy is the symbol of Bacchus, the god of wine.

18

Create an herb pillow to encourage mental alertness and impart wisdom. Stuff a six-inch-square pillow with as much dried mint as possible and stitch it up.

ABOVE: *purslane* (15) and *ivy* (17).

NOVEMBER

19

Fennel seeds should be dry by now. Fennel seed is used to help *"make thin those who are too fat"* and aid in digestion. It was also one of the herbs in an 11th century Nine-Herb Charm for curing just about anything. The other herbs were balm, pine, savory, mint, columbine, parsley, basil and thyme.

FEAST *of* ST. EDMUND
20

St. Edmund is the patron saint of sailors.
"Set garlic and beans,
at Edmund the King
The moon in the wane,
thereof hangeth a thing."

"Garlic driveth away serpents and venemous beasts."
—WILLIAM TURNER, *Herbal.* 1568

21

Sometimes this is Stir-up Sunday (the last Sunday before Advent). It is the day to make cakes to cure by Christmas. Remember, Christmas pies and cakes should be stirred clockwise only.

22

Martinmas, Old Style
Traditionally laborers returned home after a harvest with their wages. They were served huge meals. Sometimes if this day fell on Sunday it was called Split-Stomach Sunday.
"For one that is sick upon a full stomach, take fennel and chew it in thy mouth. Spit some out and take some down."
—*Fairfax Household Book*, 17th century

ST. CLEMENT'S DAY
23

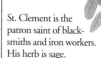

St. Clement is the patron saint of black-smiths and iron workers. His herb is sage.

24

The sun enters the house of Sagittarius. Herbs to promote the well-being of those born under the sign of Sagittarius are roses to cool and soothe headaches; they procure rest and strengthen the heart and spirit. Sage is very profitable for all pains. It helps such as are dull and heavy of spirit. Mint invigorates, chamomile takes away weariness.

ABOVE: *sage.*

NOVEMBER

ST. CATHERINE'S DAY
25

St. Catherine is the patron saint of learned men and spinsters. It is the traditional day to drink Catherine's Bowl, a highly spiced wine. *Ancient and Modern Manners of the Irish* by Camden recounts that women and girls fast on St. Catherine's Day so the girls may get good husbands and women better husbands by death or desertion of their present ones. This is the Christian version of the celebration of Nemesis, the Roman goddess of the wheel of fate.

26

New wine was tasted for the first time today. Vinalia was the ancient feast. It is a traditional time for merry-making.

27

This is the traditional time to catch eels. Make eel pie with ginger, raisins and onion, according to Mistress King's mid-17th-century receipt book.

28

This is the last day to marry before Advent.

29

It is time for the first snow.
"To make a snow tree: Take a quart of thick cream, five or six whites of eggs, a saucer of rosewater, beat them all together and as your froth riseth always take it out with a spoon. Then taken a loaf of Bread, cutaway the crust, set it in a platter and set a Rosemary bush in the midst of your loaf. Then lay your Snow-froth upon the Rosemary and so serve it."
—THOMAS JENNER,
A Book of Fruits and Flowers. 1653

ST. ANDREW'S DAY
30

St. Andrew is the patron saint of fishermen. The traditional Scots dish on this day is baked sheephead haggis and whiskey. Dill is the best herb for freshly caught fish!

ABOVE: *St. Johnswort* (27) and *savory* (28).

DECEMBER

1

"This month let thy kitchen be thy apothecary."
—Neve's *Almanack.* 1633

2

It is the traditional time to eat hutch-rabbits or "rich conies." Parsley is the herb to enhance a rabbit stew or rarebit.

3

Drinking cups made from holly wood were used to cure a lingering cough.

4

St. Barbara is the patron saint of artillerymen and those associated with explosions. *"House-leeks are good for one burned with gunpowder."*
—Hannah Woolley,
Gentlewoman's Companion. 1673

5

This is the traditional time to inspect your cider. *"Mustard will clear muddy cider,"* wrote John Newburgh in 1678 in his *Observations on Cider.*

FEAST *of* ST. NICHOLAS

6

St. Nicholas is the patron saint of children and weavers. Although the kindly saint died in the fourth century, we still put out our wooden shoes for him to fill with chocolates and golden money. For the whole Christmas season the shoes are traditionally decorated with yellow tansy buttons to symbolize the dowries in gold he provided for poor young girls, teasel for the weavers, and a carrot for the old saint's horse.

Opposite: *holly and rosemary;* above: *hemlock.*

DECEMBER

7

Rosemary is the herb of the Christmas season. *"Where rosemary grows, the woman rules the house."* The rosemary Christmas legend is that the sweet-smelling herb bloomed with white flowers until the Virgin Mary threw her blue cloak over a rosemary bush while resting on her way to Bethlehem. From that day forward the rosemary bloomed with blue flowers. A sprig of rosemary is always included in the greenery of the creche.

"A sprig of rosemary boiled in cider and drunk before bed will cure a cold."
—JOHN LLOYD'S *Book.* 1720

8

Juniper (or red cedar) is a traditional Christmas green because the Holy Family was said to have found shelter in the juniper thickets. In the Middle Ages branches were hung to fend off demons, and juniper trees were a protection from witches.

9

As we light the early fires on December evenings remember the Teutonic goddess of the hearth, Hertha. She was the source of warmth and inspiration who loved singing, and could bestow health and beauty to kindly folk. If you look carefully in the swirling woodsmoke you can see her likeness. (She is said to have a hooked nose.) Sweet dough flavored with cardamon was baked and eaten in her honor now.

10

"And here I brew both ale and wine, Now fire and hot meates thou must have December loves warme potions."
—DODOENS, 1606

11

St. Andrew's Day, Old Style

Serve fish today with dill, fennel, tarragon or bay.

ST. FINNIAN'S NIGHT

12

Never go to bed on this night without supper or you will be carried away by the fairies. Fairies abhor cumin.

ABOVE: *tarragon.*

DECEMBER

13

St. Lucy was invoked to cure eye ailments.
"HURTFUL TO EYES: *Garlic, Onion, Radish, Drunkenness, Lechery, Sweet wine Salt meats, Coleworts, Dust, Smoke, and reading presently after Supper.*
GOOD FOR EYES: *Fennel, Celandine, Eyebright, Vervain, Roses, Cloves and Cold water.*"
—WHITE'S *Almanac.* 1627

14

This is the traditional day to mark where the mistletoe grows, but never bring it into the house until Christmas Eve.

15

Today is the day to begin the mince pie season. Traditional seasonings in mincemeat are cinnamon, mace, cloves, coriander, nutmeg, pepper, brandy, lemon and orange rind.

16

The best drinks for the Christmas season are warm and spicy and should be sipped slowly.

Here is a traditional recipe for mulled wine.
"One quart of sweet red wine and ¹/₂ cup of dried herbs. Any or all of the following herbs may be used, Rosemary, Caraway, Fennel, Basil, Thyme, Ginger, Clove, Bay or Lemon balm. Heat wine until piping hot, stir in herbs with a long cinnamon stick. Steep for a half hour, strain and sip."

17

This is the day to feed your herb garden bees.
*"Go look to thy bees, if the hive be too light.
Set honey and water with rosemary dight
Which set in a dish full of sticks in the hive
From danger of famine will save them alive."*
—THOMAS TUSSER, *Five Hundred Points of Good Husbandry.* 1573

18

This was the ancient Roman holiday Ophalia that celebrated the goddess of plenty, wife of Pluto.

It is time to decorate with the holly and the ivy. Ivy is the traditional herb to wear against drunkeness. It was traditionally used to encircle the punch bowl and was often used to decorate the inn sign outside the local pub. Holly was hung over doors, windows and next to the hearth to prevent a witch from entering. The Druids held holly sacred because its leaves were ever green. Whoever first brought holly into the house ruled the household for the year.

ABOVE: *vervain.*

DECEMBER

19

The traditional Christmas drink is Wassail. Here is a traditional recipe. *"Three tart apples, two quarts apple cider, two cups orange juice, two thirds cup lemon juice, two sticks cinnamon, half teaspoon whole cloves, half teaspoon freshly grated nutmeg, half teaspoon ground allspice. Core apples, cut into rounds and bake. When they are tender and nearly brown, place in a punch bowl. Bring the other ingredients to a boil and pour over them."*

ST. THOMAS'S EVE

20

Beware of ghosts and hell-wains this night. Decorate the house with hawthorn branches as protection.

WINTER SOLSTICE / FEAST *of* ST. THOMAS

21

St. Thomas is the patron saint of masons and carpenters.

Today is the day to go caroling. In the past people went mumming on this day. They dressed in outlandish costumes with masks and went from door to door in the village presenting their neighbors with sprigs of evergreen and herbs in return for alms. This was also called "Thomasing" and "Gooding." In Scotland it was called "Hagmena" from the meaning "Holy Month."

22

The sun enters the house of Capricorn today. Herbs especially for those born under this sign include comfrey to allay the sharpness of humours, mullein to bring much ease and comfort, rosemary to calm giddiness and sharpen dullness. It helps a weak memory and procureth clear sight. Solomon's seal prevents freckles.

Capricorn was under the care of the Greek goddess Vesta.

23

Today is the day to make oneself fair for the Christmas merrymaking. Clove Water is a traditional beauty lotion. *"Mix a little Cinnamon with the Cloves, or else the Scent is apt to be too strong. Allow half a score of Cloves to a Quart of Water, let them infuse some time over hot Embers or in a warm place, then strain for use."*
—*The Cook's and Confectioner's Dictionary, or The Accomplished Housewife's Companion.* 1723

CHRISTMAS EVE

24

It is time to bring in the yule log and the mistletoe. The Christian legend is that mistletoe was once a large tree, but the cross of Christ was made from its wood, and thereafter it has been tiny and consigned to live from the charity of other trees. Sprigs of the little plant were distributed among the people to hang up in their cottages as protection and charm and as an aphrodisiac. We still kiss under the mistletoe!

The Yule Log was brought into the hall on Christmas Eve to burn through the night and into Christmas Day. It was the largest oak log possible, and it was decked with Christmas herbs.

ABOVE: *lavender.*

DECEMBER

25

The Christchild now appears in the creche or manger scene. The first creche was made by St. Francis at his hermitage high on a rock above Greccio, Italy. In a grotto the kindly saint arranged a little crib with the Holy Family around it. Peasants climbed to the grotto on Christmas when St. Francis celebrated Mass there. Italy is still known for its wonderfully elaborate creche grottoes, filled with people, animals and sweet herbs. These Christmas creche herbs are thyme, rosemary, pennyroyal, bedstraw, basil and the winter bloomimg Christmas rose. The creche spread throughout Europe and eventually developed into the Miracle Play.

26
ST. STEPHEN'S DAY / BOXING DAY

Today is the day for ex-changing gifts and beating the bushes for wrens, a custom whose beginnings are lost in the dimness of time.

ST. JOHN'S DAY
27

St. John is the patron saint of booksellers, publishers, printers and writers. His herb is costmary or bibleleaf.

Sometimes the herb is also called alecost because it was used to flavor ale and wine. The large broad leaves were pressed between the pages of a book to dry and be used as a bookmark. The scent of costmary would also prevent silverfish and bookworms. Some-times the pungent leaves were nibbled by scholars to stay awake or by church-goers to stay alert through long sermons.

CHILDERMASS
28

Childermass is the unluckiest day of the year because it was the day upon which Herod slaughtered the little children. Hang flax above the beds of children to encourage the Teutonic goddess Hulda to protect them. This was the time, in ancient days, when gods and goddesses could visit the earth. (Seven-year-old children who danced in the blue flax flowers of summer would grow up beautiful.)

29

Wassailing is in full swing. Here is an old Christmas toast:
*"Merry Christmas and Happy New Year,
Your pockets full of money and your cellars full
of beer!"*

30

Beware of eating too much Christmas chocolate today! "The confection made of Cacao called Chocolate or Chocoletto, which may be had in divers places in London at reasonable rates, is of wonderfull efficacy for the procreation of children, for it not only vehemently incites to Venus, but causeth conception in women... makes those who take it fair and amiable."
—WILLIAM COLES, *Adam in Eden.* 1657

NEW YEAR'S EVE
31

*"Happy, Happy New Year,
Till next year, till eternity,
Corn on the cornstalk,
Grapes in the vineyard, Yellow grain in the bin,
Red apples in the garden, Silkworms in the house,
Happiness and health Until next year."*
—ADELMA SIMMONS, *Merry Christmas Herbal,* Translated from the Bulgarian.

ABOVE: *rosemary.*